Bygone Whitehaven

Volume Five

by Michael and Sylvia Moon

*A photographic look at life
in Whitehaven over
the last one hundred years.*

Michael Moon's Bookshop,
41, 42 & 43 Roper Street,
Whitehaven,
Cumbria.

For Douglas Christopher Moon, born 17th July 1983 – one of the newer Whitehaven 'fellas'.

ISBN 0-904131-28-9

Designed and printed by
Smith Settle, Otley, West Yorkshire

Cover illustration: See page 22.

Introduction

It is a nice feeling when someone stops you in the street and says 'My Dad was on the front cover of your last book', or when a lady says 'I showed my daughter a picture of me in a Victory Parade, waving a flag, as a young school girl'. We have always said that the history of a town is embodied in the people who live there. Without the townspeople there would be no one for politicians and spokesmen to mould and influence. Parents and Grandparents are as much part of our town's recent past as any member of the landed gentry – usually more so – since they resided here all the time.

If you see a few familiar faces in this fifth volume in the series, well and good. If you don't it is because you have not looked through your family albums and chocolate boxes of old snaps. We hope to get enough material to compile volume six, but we will really need your help to do it. Happy reading.

Michael and Sylvia Moon
Whitehaven, September 1984.

Acknowledgements

We would like to take this opportunity to thank the many people at home and abroad who have helped us with pictures and advice for this book. Mrs M. Collis, Mr and Mrs Lucas, Dick Bewsher, Mr and Mrs Graham, Mr E. G. Robertson, Inspector Reay, E. Lamb & Son, Nathan C. Bie, Miss Janette Crichton, Mrs James, Mrs Mabel Scott, Mrs G. Thomson, Miss E. Bell, Mr T. Durham, Mr Hickson, Mrs E. Moses, Copeland Council, Mr Harry Fancy, Mrs Inglesfield, Mrs Mary Kelley of Toronto and Mrs Gordon Stamp of Scarborough, Ontario, and the many other people who encouraged us to compile this fifth book in the series.

Recent Changes

Many areas of town have undergone changes since our last book. Some businesses have closed for a variety of reasons, properties have become unsafe and have had to be demolished and much important new building work has been undertaken. These changes alter the visual landscape of the town and here we record some of the larger ones.

Demolished: The Old Infirmary, Howgill Street.
Harry S. Taylor's Warehouse, Queen Street.
The Oddfellows' Hall, Lowther Street.
Block of shops, Tangier Street.
The Queen's Cinema.
Old Cottages, Howgill Street.
Finlay's Tobacconists opposite the Bus Station.

New Building Work:
Extensive new housing development between George Street and Duke Street for B.N.F.L.
The Golden Lion in the Market Place – virtually rebuilt for B.N.F.L.
Doctors' Surgery, 1 Lowther Street – extensively refurbished and extended.
Ray's Dental Surgery, Scotch Street – externally refurbished.
Dixon's Superstore, Lowther Street.
Ashbridge's Butchers, King Street.
Bradford and Bingley Building Society – knocked down their old offices and replaced it with a dressed-stone building in keeping.
Paved area with seats, trees and cast-iron lamp-posts in Queen Street.
New shop from an old derelict warehouse at the end of Lowther Street for Northern Rock.
Refurbishment of the old Steel's Motor Bike shop into Nightclub and multiple uses at Tangier Street.
Refurbishment of the old Routledge block of shops in James Street.
Refurbishment of Somerset House in Duke Street.
New Supermarket for Presto on the site of the old Queen's Cinema.
New Sub-Divisional Police Station (the one with the peculiar shaped windows) on the site of the old Congregational Church.
Old Billiard Hall, Coates Lane, rebuilt as two shops for Ian Kyle, Barber.

Lost Businesses:
Burnyeat's Sports Shop, Lowther Street.
Callander and Dixon's Stationers, King Street.
George Todd and Son, Printers, Marlborough Street.
Stout's Foundry, New Town – the last local Foundry.
Stout's Garage, Roper Street.
King's Saleroom, Roper Street, now part of Moon's Bookshop.
Williams' Ladies Outfitters, Duke Street – retired.
Pond's Grocers, Duke Street – now Mitchell's Auction Company's office.
Peeney's Fish and Chip Shop – now a Chinese Take-Away.

These have a questionable future:
The Old Town Hall, empty and becoming unsafe.
The Court Offices, Scotch Street, to close.
The Globe Hotel, empty and becoming an eyesore.

Milestones:
Thomas Roe's Provision Merchants known locally as Tommy Roe's Bacon Shop celebrates its centenary this year. The family have been in continuous occupation of the building and the business since 1884. Well Done.

In 1923 when this photo was taken, local motor-driven omnibuses were still something of a novelty. Many people had never ridden on one of these new-fangled machines. The 'bus ride was a little rougher than we are used to today – with its solid rubber tyres and crank starting handle. This passenger vehicle, one of the earliest 'buses to be owned by Cumberland Motor Services, was driven by Mr Tom Dent who is seen here standing with his conductor, by the side of the 'bus. The registration number of this 'bus was AO 6009.

The Queen's Cinema was the brainwave of a local Pork Butcher, Sammy West, who noticed the popularity of Moving Pictures which attracted regular crowds to the Market Hall Picture Palace and St. James' Hall. He bought an old almost derelict warehouse in Swingpump Lane, little used other than by a Brigade Band who practiced in the room to the right of the archway. The building was being held together with layer upon layer of posters. Mr West did much of the hard work of demolition himself, and erected a building behind the warehouse shell and remodelled the front extensively in the grandiose cinema style of the day. It was ready for public performances by 1928, and the last photo in this sequence, (on page 8), kindly lent by his daughter Mrs James, shows the building ready for the first performance. We well remember the sign on the wall downstairs 'This Cinema is Sprayed Daily with Chromosol'. After it ceased to be used as a cinema, it became a Bottle Recovery Depot and in early 1984 was pulled down along with part of the adjoining Catholic Chapel to enable Presto Supermarkets to build a new large grocery store.

8

Mr West was not a member of a cinema or theatrical family. Rather he was an entrepreneur who saw a local need and did his best to meet it. He was specifically a Pork and Pork Products Butcher and ran this well-known shop in the Market Place. The hard physical work in the mines, dock and factories done by local people meant that they needed good square meals with plenty of meat. There were many butchers around at the time. This one is Hinde and Trafford's shop at No.54 King Street – now long gone.

Marathons and Fun Runs are not new. What Whitehaven did 70 years ago, the rest of the country eventually gets round to imitating. These two published post-cards show the start and finish of the Whitehaven Walking Competition. It started in the Market Place and finished at the Grand Hotel by Bransty Railway Station. It certainly brought out the crowds.

We all now live in the Copeland District Council area. It used to be the Borough of Whitehaven. This picture, taken in 1894, shows the Mayor Making Ceremony at the Town Hall when the Rt. Hon. Hugh Cecil, Earl of Lonsdale was installed as the First Mayor of the Borough.

Sadly the Town Hall is in a poor state of repair these days. It is now empty and the Council Offices are now in Catherine Street. Large pieces of the cement rendering have fallen off the front of the building. It used to be called The Cupola and was very much in evidence on Matthias Read's celebrated Bird's Eye View of Whitehaven engraved in 1738, so the building itself is of great antiquity. At present without an occupant, no buyer in sight and no obvious use, it may well be demolished.

At a time of inflation and high unemployment, and with the prospect of the final shut down of the last surviving pit in the County looming large, let us hark back to better days when the town was pleased to put out the flags. We put them out for a Victory March at the end of the First World War and the Town Band and the Fire Brigade marched through the streets. Here you can see the procession marching up Tangier Street at Whittle's corner. We might have won the war, but we lost too many fathers, brothers, sons and breadwinners.

We also decked out the streets with bunting for the Coronation of King Edward VII in 1902. A double celebration in a way. The King had been taken ill with appendicitis in June, and the original date of the coronation June 26th had to be postponed. Fortunately, His Majesty made a good recovery and the ceremony was rescheduled for August 9th. Having an appendix removed may seem a very commonplace operation these days with wonderful anaesthetics but 82 years ago it was a very different story. This scene shows a procession moving up Lowther Street, past Moss's with its royal crown outside and the Midland Bank across the road.

The lower snapshot sent to us from Mrs Mary Kelley of Toronto was taken by her father Mr James Ellwood of 25 Church Street to show her the bunting put up for the Silver Jubilee Celebrations of King George V and Queen Mary. A view of Lother Street with the Oddfellows' Hall on the left (recently taken down), and the old Jennings House The Whittington Cat before it was given a new frontage.

Local Booksellers seem to be a dying breed these days. We have just seen, at the beginning of 1984, the demise of Callander and Dixon after more than a century and a half, though latterly, under new ownership, it ceased to be a bookshop in its old sense. Adair's, Moss's, Burlington's have all gone now – as families grew old and retired the premises were redeveloped or altered to other trades. This faded photo of Burlington's Booksellers and Newsagents at 63 Lowther Street was taken around the turn of the century. A much loved and well-remembered shop, it was taken down in the late 1960's and the Coal Board and Pearl Assurance Offices built on the site.

W. H. Smith and Son are probably the best known newsagents and booksellers in the country with hundreds of branches in most of the larger towns, cities and railway stations. This picture of their old premises on King Street, now Cowpe's Curtain Centre was taken before the last War. There is a poster for the newly published 'The Prince of Wales Gift Book' in the window, which dates the picture nicely. Pictured here are two attractive lady assistants who have stepped outside to have their pictures taken. The old image of the small local W. H. Smith branches has long since gone. The branches at Cockermouth and Workington have closed, and in other places you can now go into their large stores, for that is what they have become, for a quick warm on a cold day and get anything from a pencil to a calculator, from a music cassette to a computer – and all self-service too!

The Prince of Wales came to West Cumberland in 1927. Here he is being introduced to some of the Officials of Haig Pit. He has just shaken hands with Tom Durham, the Mine Agent. The Mayor, well known Confectioner Sammy Turner is checking 'who is who' on his list and hoping he won't have to use his umbrella. Some of these men were killed not long afterwards investigating a pit explosion.

Many souvenir pieces of pottery were sold locally to commemorate the Royal Visit. Although it isn't generally known these pieces of transfer printed pottery were the first to be issued depicting the Prince of Wales' portrait. The Monarchy did very little visiting outside London and most of the people in Great Britain had never seen any Royalty at all. These items, issued in Egremont, Whitehaven, Cleator Moor and Distington, are from our own collection.

If you wanted a special cake for a celebration such as a wedding or anniversary you usually went to Batty's to order it. M. A. Batty's Confectioners at 14 Lowther Street was *the* place to go to. All the visiting dignitaries used to go there – no Westlands Hotel before the War. The Prince of Wales went for his lunch there. The business was run very successfully by Mrs Nixon of Moss Bank, a lady who many will remember. In the late 1960's Cyril Moore absorbed the shop into his Furniture Business and, more recently Donald Dixon swallowed the lot. The two shop views of Batty's date from the turn of the century.

The Theatre Royal is no more. But the tradition of public entertainment continues on the site as our Antiquarian Bookshop is there! Interior views of actual performances taken under difficult lighting conditions are rarely come across. We are indebted to Mr E. G. Robertson for this photo of the W.A.O.S. Players on stage in Gilbert and Sullivan's 'The Gondoliers' at the Finale of Act One, taken in 1923.   **19**

Good musicals needed good accompaniment and here we see the Theatre Royal Orchestra under the leadership of Mr Alfred Robertson A.R.C.O., Musical Director, taken in the 1920's. Mr Cowper on double base, Mrs Ives in black lace dress was the pianist, Alvyn Hunter on violin and William Watson clarinettist. Mr Robertson's son supplied some of the details – you, Dear Reader, will probably tell us the rest.

Local theatre-goers were in a fortunate situation in the 1920's with a thriving Amateur Operatic Society and the Theatre Royal in Roper Street in which to put on their performances. The Group put on many memorable costume dramas and light operas. This picture dated April 1928 shows the cast of 'My Lady Molly'. Quite a few well-known faces here.

All L-R: *Back row:* Tom Lawson (Joiner), Jack Wattleworth.
Middle row: John Singleton (Solicitor) – Treasurer and Business Manager,
Louie Ramsay (now Mrs Tom McKay), Alan Wilson (Dentist), Arthur Wilson
(Dentist – son of Alan Wilson), Dr E. H. 'Teddy' Ablett (Hon. Secretary).
Dorothy Field, Alfred Robertson – Musical Director.
Front row: Tom Glaister, Annie Turner, Margaret 'Maggie' Ramsay, Jack Backhouse.

The players retired to the old Grand Hotel on Saturday after the Matinee for tea and fortification before the evening performance, and it was outside the Grand Hotel that the group photos were usually taken. This one is by the Romney Studios.

Musical Memories. We are indebted to Mrs Mabel Scott for giving us this lovely group photograph of the Colliery Mission Band of Hope in Rosemary Lane. Her father, George Mason is the little fellow sitting to the left of the big drum, though it is doubtful that he played it, since it was bigger than he was. The picture was taken in 1906, when George was 4 years old. Now over 82 years old and a retired Glazier, he had a lifelong interest in sport. He took a keen interest in Amateur Football, playing with the Whitehaven Corinthians in the mid-1920's and later coaching with the High Duty Alloys A.F.C. after the last War. There must be quite a few Grandads on this picture. I wonder how many recognise

themselves?

In 1934 the ship The Iron Duke paid a good-will visit to the Town and the Proprietor of Haig
Pit, Mr Priestman, invited them to go down the mine and see what the sea looked like from
underneath. As they all look remarkably clean we can only assume that this picture must
have been taken before the descent. Mr Priestman is in the middle, Tom Banks, the Mine
Manager is on the extreme left next to Tom Durham.

Few businesses survived from the eighteenth century into the twentieth century. Probably the only local survivor nowadays is Jefferson's the Lowther Street Wine Merchants who will celebrate their 200th anniversary in 1985. Charlie Gordon's Ironmongers came into this exclusive bracket with a year to spare, being founded in 1799. it was situated at No.32 King Street where the Motorist Discount Centre is today. How many Sports shops do you know which sell hammers and chisels? Not many! But on the other hand how many Ironmongers can you bring to mind with a Sports Department? This pleasantly surprising window display reveals all. In the left-hand window are goods for Golf, Tennis, Cricket and Croquet – materials for the upper-crust. Whilst in the other were forks and shovels for the peasantry. An assortment of different sizes of watering can and a wooden rollered mangle – once so common, but now almost completely replaced by the washing machine and spin dryer. (We have four old wooden rollered mangles ourselves – but we do not take in washing, well at least we haven't had to up to now!)

Lonsdale Place – a very long time ago. When did you last see ladies dressed like these? The iron railing round the front gardens disappeared during the last war. This fine row of property used to look out over green hills. There was no estate on Bransty then and no heavy traffic coming from the Loop Road which was still a long way off being constructed. A bit of a pull for chaps on bikes though!

Even more of a 'pull' if you went to do your courting on either of these contraptions. The 'Penny Farthing' was probably a Singer Xtra-ordinary Penny Farthing of 1879 and the Tri-cycle dates from 1880. Would you dare ride it down Inkermann Terrace? Only a deaf man would brave the light-hearted heckles if he rode it through the Ginns!

In this country we never seem to be prepared for bad weather. It always comes as a total shock when it snows. This is a wintery scene about 1908, looking down Inkermann Terrace with the old St. Nicholas Church Vicarage bifurcating the road. The gas lamp has been changed and there are now no notices forbidding the riding of bicycles down Front Corkicle, but when all you had to watch out for were horse-drawn carriages it was a different matter. The cast iron Pillar-Box erected during the reign of Edward VII survives – we still use it regularly.

And yet more snow at the New Road, with traffic reduced to a single Horse and Cart. This picture was taken in the 1920's.

We always try and include something nautical in our books and we have searched the National Press for this example which was featured in The Graphic in July, 1871. It depicts the launching of The Patterdale from the yard of the Whitehaven Shipbuilding Company. It weighed in at 1187 tons and was the first ship that this company had built.

Occasionally we get very severe winds which do much damage to buildings and property. The sea is whipped up into fantastic white breakers which cascade over the lighthouses and come crashing over the sea walls. In 1927 a string of coal waggons was blown off the railway lines and into the dock. Gale force winds in January of 1984 brought chunks of Harry S. Taylor's Warehouse in Queen Street crashing through the roof of next-door property, whilst chimneys fell through the roof and masonry crashed to the street round the Oddfellows' Hall – both have since been demolished. The Taylor property, an old bonded-warehouse was much the older building, the Oddfellows' Hall designed by J. S. Shepherd was only approved for building in 1887 so failed to reach its century – something not common in the town centre. The ornamental cresting was taken down with a view to incorporating it into another building on the site, though this would not be easy.

MARRIED ON THE HIGH SEAS.
Capᵗⁿ Schröder to Caroline Schultze
on board the "BORWICK RAILS," off Whitehaven
May 27ᵗʰ 1911.

Speaking of high seas brings us round to this most unusual postcard. We have seen cards of blind musicians, a pet goose, a piano playing midget, flagdays and street scenes, but would you send your friends a picture of the wedding of total strangers – not even British strangers, who were married at sea? This postcard depicts a Norwegian Captain of the Steamship 'Riim' Captain Schröder who married Caroline Schultze on board the Tugboat 'Borwick Rails' on the 'high seas' outside the three mile limit in the Solway Firth, off the coast of Whitehaven in May 1911. Why did he marry her there? Well quite simply, the Captain after having the Banns read in Norway had to get back to his ship and could not stay in any one place long enough to fulfill the residence qualification. After talks with the Norwegian Consul in Liverpool he arranged to be married 'on the high seas' by the Whitehaven Presbyterian Minister, The Rev. Matthew Young. The bride could speak no English so the ship's mate translated. The Chairman of The Harbour Commissioners Ald. W. McGowan JP was present wearing his flat cap and a good overcoat. The boat came back into the Wet Dock and by this time 200 people had gathered on the quayside to welcome the couple back, from whence they alighted to go for luncheon at the Grand Hotel.

One of the more spectacular and costly renovations of recent years in town has been the complete restoration (some said it was more like a resurrection) of the whole block of houses and shop known as Singleton's Corner – opposite the Whitehaven News Offices in Roper Street. This lovely picture shows the three ladies who ran this well-known Bakers and Confectionery Business. It was taken in 1936. Do you remember the enamelled white letters for Fry's Milk Chocolate which were stuck on every corner shop window in the kingdom? Millions upon millions of these letters were produced by enamel sign makers and being almost indestructable they survived – glued like limpets for years. Even when they fell off, or were rubbed off by frustrated window cleaners, in certain lights the ghostly image of the missing letters would still spell out the words, bleached into the very material of the glass by the sun and the rain. The shop was recently 'Patchouli's' an up-market dress shop and is now a sports goods shop called Olympic Way, run by the Nelson family, and fulfilling a need left by the demise of the Burnyeat Business in the same line.

World War Two. 10th November 1940. The Civil Defence First Aid Centre was situated in the old Hospital in Howgill Street and this picture taken by Bryan Smith of seven attractively-clad young ladies in their wellies, oilskins and tin helmets and first aid kits, was taken on the steps of the old Central School. The ladies are: Elizabeth Hornsley, Mary Johnson, Theresa Carling, E. Payton, J. Wilson, M. Lofthouse and Miss Janette Crichton. Miss Crichton worked for Smith Brothers and remained a member of this service until she joined the R.A.F. It is not easy to be ladylike in this garb, but they obviously did their best, didn't they?

This picture and the one which follows have been sent to us all the way from Canada by one of the people who appears in the pictures – Mr Gordon Stamp.

West Cumberland's first Animal Clinic at 24 Queen Street, seen here in 1939 at the beginning of the War. The property was originally Coomb's Grocers and was renovated and opened in May 1937 by Mr Stamp's father – the late Captain Frederick E. Stamp (nicknamed 'The Major'), as a Free Animal Clinic. He served the community as its Inspector of Cruelty, Acting Secretary, Part-time Veterinarian and Branch Organiser for the R.S.P.C.A. His son Gordon was the Clinic Manager. The windows used to be filled with packets of foreign stamps and many a lad got the philately bug from packets bought here.

West Cumberland's one and only R.S.P.C.A. A.R.P. Mobile Unit (actually a 1937 Austin 7 car) for the purpose of salvaging livestock for human consumption after air-raids (which fortunately we never got). The picture was taken just above No.6 Corkickle, which was the residence of 'The Major' and Branch Office. A set of surgical equipment any hospital would be proud of, the holstered gun and a snare are not part of usual hospital equipment these days. Gordon's mother Florence is wearing the starched nurse's uniform. A most unusual family group photograph, certainly for our books. Thank you Mr Gordon Stamp for sending it to us.

Alfred Barlow's Ironmongers of 25 Lowther Street. A picture taken about 1912 when it was still quite a new business. A very full window indeed. Hardware and Household Utensils at Lowest Prices. Repairs promptly attended to, and a large selection of pocket penknives and scissors always in stock. Mr Barlow eventually took over the premises to the left of the picture – Mr Partington's Butchers shop which we featured on page 33 of volume four of this modest series. Notice the attractive ornamental awning.

Where do these photographs come from? I hear you ask. A variety of sources, but this must be the strangest to date – from under the glass top of an old cast-iron public house beer table. We bought the top without the legs only to find that there were not one but two rounds of photographic advertisements one on top of the other showing local businesses. This idea nowadays is perpetuated in the Rugby Team Fixture Calendars you see hung up in Chip Shops. The Barlow's shop is no more, last year it became yet another Building Society Office.

In this book you will find all the energetic sports – walking, cycling, football, tennis, banging a big drum and getting married at sea. This group photograph shows a more relaxing past-time, a Bowls Competition organised at the Whitehaven Bowls Club in 1922, between the Businessmen and Shopkeepers. There must be a few well-known faces here. Do

you recognise anyone?

The late Dick Bewsher, taxi driver at Bie and Conaway's Station Garage in 1931. Dick is standing in mackintosh and peaked cap beside one of their Austin Taxis. This vehicle was bought secondhand from Mr McCowan of Roseneath – General Manager of The Coke Ovens. It had a 20 gallon petrol tank and did only 12 miles to the gallon, at a time when petrol was under a shilling a gallon.

The Garage housed six taxis and the firm had four other vehicles housed elsewhere. Fares were two shillings in town, half a crown to Kells and Hensingham, five shillings to St. Bees and ten shillings to Workington – which was nearly half a week's wages. The service was used mainly by train passengers who alighted at Bransty Station weighed down with luggage, or Reps. with trade samples.

Adam Thwaites was their mechanic – by trade a blacksmith. He and Dick kept the vehicles serviced and running. If a part broke – Adam would make one. In an age when few people owned their own cars, most people would only travel in a vehicle such as this to weddings and funerals. The cars were any colour you liked as long as it was black. Huge though this vehicle looked they owned an even larger one: a 20 h.p. Sunbeam, for example, which did only 5 miles to the gallon. Healthy competition was provided by the rival taxi firm at Central Garage Duke Street which was run by Roy Eynon.

On a warm summer's evening it was nice to take the family to St. Bees after an afternoon's ride around the Lakes. The people could stretch their legs, eat J. K. Lee's St. Bega brand of Treacle Toffee and take in the ozone. The cars would all be parked on the dunes. The little hut is where the Beach Shop is situated today. The photo was taken pre-war.

From St. Bees to Charles Bie in one quick step brings us back into the centre of town and a memory of one of the best known Boot and Shoe Businesses which even today after the Bie family has retired from business still bears the name Charles Bie.

Charles Bie who died in 1928, founded the business which bore his name in 1909. He was born in 1865 in the village of the Isle of Whithorn in Wigtownshire. He was the eldest of eight sons and he was taken to sea, under his father, in the family Brig which traded amongst the various ports around the Solway Firth. One day whilst the ship was in Harrington Charles declined further employment with his father and 'jumped ship'. He came to Whitehaven and apprenticed himself to Wallace Brothers of 75 Market Place, Wholesale and Retail Boot and Shoe Manufacturers and his indenture paper dated October 11th 1882 still survives. It shows that he was to receive 8/- a week for the first year rising to 12/- a week for his third year. Until he was able to support himself his mother sent money across to him. In 1890 he was appointed manager to the local branch of Stead & Simpson shoe dealers (see picture) and this post he held for 19 years until he opened his own shoe business at 70 King Street in 1909. Ten years later he transferred his growing business to 80 King Street and there by chance he traded next door to Wallace's then at 79a King Street with whom he had served his apprenticeship 37 years earlier. In 1924, just after the fearful depression which befell the Country after the First World War, he moved the business to its present address 19 Lowther Street. After Mr Bie's death in 1928, the business was continued by his widow and youngest son, Nathan Bie, who in turn took his wife into partnership after the death of his mother in 1944. Mr Albert Carey who entered the firm in 1929, on leaving school, conducted the business as Junior Partner after the retirement of Mr and Mrs Bie from active participation in 1971. He had a large staff of nine well-trained shoe fitters. The business still trades under the name of its founder, 75 years and hundreds of thousands of pairs of shoes later.

With a new Presto Supermarket being built on the old Queen's Cinema site and the recent takeover of the W.B.G. Superstore at Hillcrest by Lipton's we are getting nearer the time when there will be no small Grocers left at all in town. Roe's Bacon Shop must be a rare exception, this year it celebrates its 100th birthday of trading from its Duke Street address. We wish them well towards their double century. This picture is of one of the many small grocers which have sunk without trace. Ferguson and Bell's Grocers of 21 Church Street (between where Lakeland Laundry and Carron's Insurance are today). The picture shows Mr Bell and his assistant Miss Elsie Wilson and was taken 63 years ago in 1921. Mahogany topped counter piled high with packets of Scott's Porridge Oats, white apron at the ready, their blends of tea advertised from 1/4 to 2/4 a POUND, and Oxo's at 50 for 4/-. You can just see the bentwood chair to the left of the picture for customers to sit on. When did you last see your Grocer wearing a flat cap . . . indoors that is. Perhaps we could start a new

fashion?

Also rescued from the beer table top was this picture of Ernest Lamb and Son, Outfitters, Tailors, Hatters and Hosiers at No.6 King Street. Suits to order from 20/-, trousers from 7/6, at the time they also had a branch at Workington. The well-known sign reproduced here was their slogan for years . . . the sign had the back of the head on both sides. Messrs Lamb founded in 1905, moved down to their present address in the early 1920's. It is still a family run business, 79 years and 4 generations later.

Walker's Tannery on Scotch Street about 1900. Before the age of plastic and synthetic rubber, leather played a very important part in everyday life in the home and in commerce. It is hard to think of an activity in which leather did not play a part. It was used for belts, as part of men's braces, for boot and shoe soles and uppers, not to mention laces, clogs, razer strops, bicycle saddles, washers for bike pumps and water taps, for luggage-suitcases and hatboxes, for harness, saddles, reins, carriage seating, chair upholstery, whips, protective gloves and aprons, miner's knee pads, leather belting for driving steam powered machinery in factories and mills to name but a few. The raw hides were dipped into various vats of powerful liquids which cleaned, softened and preserved the skins which were scraped with wide bladed spokeshaves to remove hair and bristles. The hair was used for upholstering furniture and the bristles for brushes. The smell from these processes must have been pretty pungent. Early interior photographs are rare and particularly of industrial processes – these must be over 80 years old. The building is almost unrecognisable today. Much was demolished and what is left forms part of Bill Brown's Motor Cycle Store on High Street, a centre for the 'leather boys' of today. The Walker's home was at Oaklea and is better known **42** by its new name The Chase Hotel.

Sunday isn't Sunday without a visit to Church – it makes a positive start to the week and gives one a time to quietly reflect what happened in the working week just past. This 75 year old photograph puzzled us for some time as we could not place the buildings beside St. James' Church at all, until we realized that a photographer had made a print with the negative the wrong way round. For you, Dear Reader, we have corrected that error. But if you want a surprise try looking at it through a mirror.

Another picture of High Street, issued as a postcard showing the Church and solid town
houses from the well-tended gardens across the road in 1905 long before the present
46 St. James' Infant School was built.

The next five pictures are taken from rare tiny carte-de-visite photographs of various local subjects taken about 1865. They are all taken by some anonymous person who wrote ink captions on the back. It is possible he lived at Rosehill and was a keen amateur photographer as we have seen pictures taken of that particular house both inside and out in this same batch.

The first four Sergeants in The Whitehaven Rifles circa 1865.

A view of the Brickworks with nothing in sight but green pastures – no Mirehouse and not much of Hensingham by the look of it.

St. James' Church decorated for Christmas 1865. Note the controversial pulpit and the two side windows beside the altar which are now bricked up. The decorative plasterwork ceiling at least has survived intact.

55 Duke Street from near where the Public Baths now stand. Note particularly the tall warehouse on the left almost opposite the Globe Hotel. This warehouse was acquired and altered by The Cleator Moor Co-operative Society. A date appears on the facade – 1858 – today, but this refers to the date of the founding of The Society not the building itself, which is much older and when this picture was taken had more floors in it. It is a long time since stage-coaches parked there. It has recently become a very busy building . . . a nightclub, fun-pub, takeaway food centre and a kitchen centre. The kind of intensive building use, Whitehaven rarely ever sees.

A picture from the 1860's of the Royal Standard on the Docks with many buildings beyond and a large chimney *(now demolished)*.

This picture of the Staff of the Whitehaven Infirmary at the Castle in Flatt Walks was found in a Flea Market by us and shows the Nursing and Medical Staff of the newly opened building taken some time in 1926. All starched aprons and split-shifts in those days. The only person we have been able to identify is Dr Muriel, sitting to Matron's right. It must have been quite an improvement to working at the old Howgill Street Infirmary. Looking through old newspapers we found a cutting showing the proposed site of a new hospital at Hensingham, dated as far back as 1939, so this newly altered building must have been **50**   thought of as a stopgap measure even then.

The old Infirmary in Howgill Street had a variety of uses after the hospital use ceased there, it became a school, shirt factory and printing works but disappeared quietly without a fuss in 1982. We took these and other pictures of its demolition. At present it is being well used as a Car Park – still serving the needs of the community.

Central Music Stores Duke Street. The business was started by Richard Laurie Brooks in 1922. A window full of ukeleles and big horned gramophones and Mr Brooks was offering copies of the latest comedy fox-trot record called Shanghai for two shillings. This later, rescued, snapshot dates from the early 1930's. It shows the enlarged frontage of the business now called R. L. Brooks Central Music Stores. Next door at No.97 The Mart was the premises of Jackson and Murray which did not come down as we said in volume 4 but was taken over by Brooks and Jackson & Murray moved into part of the new Empress Building and stayed there until September 1984 when they quietly moved across the road into Pond's old shop at 17A Duke Street.

1984 will go down in history as the time of probably the bitterest strike in the Coal Industry which at the time of writing has just passed the six month mark. Haig Pit is virtually now closed for good and from over the sea in Toronto we are sent some particularly apt pictures of miners during a strike in May 1921 digging for coal at Scilly Banks in a field behind Hope Hall (where open-cast mining has been operating for some two years). The coal was dug out to a depth of 19 feet using tree branches as a primitive form of crane and windlass. Concern was being expressed by miners at a meeting at the Colliery Recreation Ground reported the local press at the time that coal was being mined and sold to keep industrial concerns supplied with coal. The idea that the coal was merely for home consumption seemed not to have been entirely true, though it is hard for us to realise these days with alternative sources of power that not too long ago everything was heated and cooked on an open fire. The ever enterprising Mr James Bellman took the photographs. Mrs Mary Kelley formerly of Whitehaven and now well into her 80's, living in Canada, sent us these poignant pictures, which we had not seen before.

We have a thriving soap powder and detergent making industry in the Marchon Chemical Co. now called Albright and Wilson at Kells. But who can tell us where this brand of soap was made locally? Called FERFEX 'well begun half done' was the catchphrase used to sing its praises. This early showcard coloured in red, green and black was found in the back of an old picture frame where it had been used as a stiffener. It is obviously quite old, from the style of costume and lettering it is probably before the First World War. Does anyone know where it was made, or better still has anyone got a packet? We have a wooden case full of blocks of Monkey Brand Soap which everyone over the age of 50 will know . . . 'Monkey Brand Soap – will not wash clothes'. It was used as a block abrasive scourer for cleaning metal-ware such as brass and copper.

This is another Cumberland 'bus, again the same driver as before Mr Tom Dent, standing by AO6652 Bus No.5, decked out with flowers and chintz curtains for Workington Shopping Week in 1924. We still decorate 'buses today by turning them into one big moving advertisement. One particular firm pays for the whole 'bus to be painted in a style of livery to suit their own image, as these vary greatly it can be confusing trying to see if the red 'bus you are waiting for, which turns out to be blue is the same 'bus you want to travel on.

The Whitehaven Corinthians Football Team for the year 1924 – 1925. Eleven men and a reserve. Mr George Mason is on the back row at the left. You will remember he was the little lad by the Colliery Mission Band big drum . . . didn't he grow!

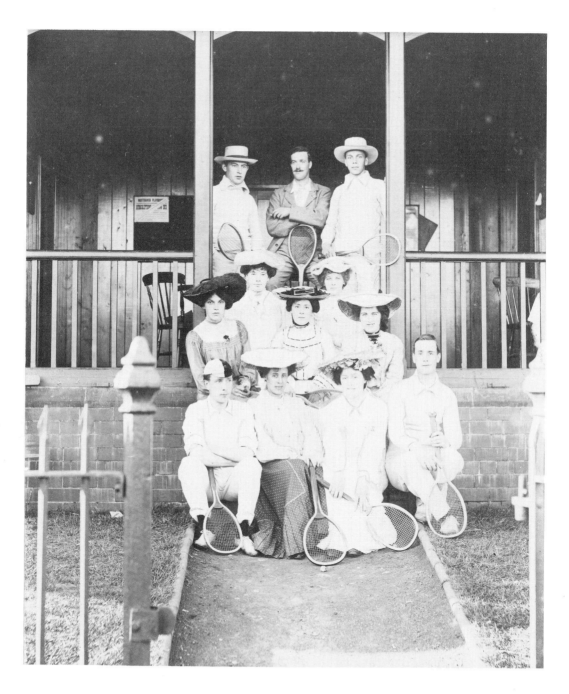

Whitehaven Social Tennis Club Team for the season of 1904. A dignified bunch with long skirts and big hats for ladies and the men with long flannels and panama hats except the chap in the two-tone cap on the front row who was a member of the Collis family of Pawnbrokers – father of the late Cyril Collis. I wonder what McEnroe would have made of it all? Notice how the racquets have changed shape over the intervening years. The photograph was taken by Leech of Kells.

We watch sport on television and we can listen to it on the radio, even whilst driving around in a car or lorry. It hasn't always been as simple as this. Just look at this lovely little snap of a man with his homemade set put together on the front parlour table. Wireless was still fun in the late 20's when you had to build your own sets using big valves and batteries. This picture was found on the floor of a local saleroom and rescued by us. The man in the picture could be a member of the Thorpe Ironmongers family.

These two Carnival snaps were kindly lent us by Mrs Elsie Moses. The first shows a Hospital float in the Whitehaven Hospital Carnival of 1932, her father is standing in front of the decorated shire horse.

In the lower snap taken the following year 1933 he is standing with a walking stick, with two other men in front of the William Pit Float which has a scale model of the pit surface buildings and the slogan that people should use local coal. Mrs Moses' father was Thomas Henry Cannon of Bransty – a winner of the 'Pitman's V.C.'

This is a particularly attractive harbour scene issued as a postcard locally between the wars and printed by W. H. Smith. The becalmed vessel reminds one of the nineteenth century Dutch seascape pictures which often showed boats like this.

King Street after the last war. Timothy Whites and Taylors Chemists can be clearly seen on the left hand corner, now a fast food pie and sandwich takeaway. E. K. Lees well-known shop on the right and Edgards further up the street.

This photo was taken on the steps of the Town Hall on the occasion of the laying of the Memorial Stone of the 1,000th house erected by Whitehaven Corporation; the ceremony was performed by G. H. Shakespeare, Esq., M.A., M.P., Parliamentary Secretary to the Ministry of Health, on July 28th 1933. The Mayor was William Rowe. After the photo was taken the group went by luxury Cumberland saloon 'bus to the Woodhouse Number Two Housing Site where the stone was formally laid. Now, with a change in housing policy, people who have paid rent for years can, if they so wish, buy the property they live in and become owners rather than occupiers. The remarkable recent transformations which can be seen all over the housing estates are a great visual improvement to the housing landscape. **63**

We always end our books with a plea for help for our next book, and this is no exception. What we have done is to show you how the seemingly commonplace snapshot can show things we have no record of otherwise. Mrs Elsie Moses showed us this photograph of her two children Geoff and Jean taken in 1955 outside the Preston Street Whitehaven Auction Mart. Nothing unusual so far but look at the block of property on the right: this whole block of three storeyed property has come down and we have never seen any pictures of it before. The date 1955 means we know it was still standing then, but what is there now . . . nothing but a car park and a fenced off piece of weed-covered land, next door to the now de-consecrated Christ Church. A town's history is brought alive from visual clues like these. Have you any which help expand the story of our favourite town?